MOTIVATIONAL WORDS

NIZA FAYAZ

Made with ♥ on the Notion Press Platform
www.notionpress.com

Contents

Contents

Preface

She says- I planned to write a motivational piece of writing, from the day she recognised she has a talent of writing.
What made her to choose write the motivational poetry is everyone tried to push her back but she believed herself.

Acknowledgements

Niza Fayaz is the youngest writer who recognised her talent of writing in her 5th grade. But what stopped her from publishing her piece of writing earlier is there was none to motivate her more but she motivated herself by her own positive self.

She wants to be a cardiologist in her future life, But writing is her passion.

She has 3 more siblings, two sisters and one brother.

She says there were only 2 people in her life who always supported her and are supporting her, they are her strength, Her parents, Tahira Maqbool and Fayaz Ahmad Bhat.

Her dream is to provide every comfort to her parents.

1. The Different Hours

Some day the hour comes,
That makes me one of those some,
whose mind is full of nothing but fun.
Being one among those some l,
Is the hour of being me,
And so free.
And then the hour comes,
That makes me one of those some,
Whose mind is full of thoughts and doubts,
Being one among those some,
Is the hour of being all for myself,
Me and my pen and paper.
And then the hour comes,
That makes me one of those some,
Who are being subjucated by them,
Being one among those some,
Is the hour of being dumb,
And then I put their lips on gum,
And then again I get the glimplse of fun.
And then the hour comes,
That makes me one of those some,
Who are so stressed and depressed,
And then by gods grace,

I am being blessed by many things,
to be impressed.
And then comes the hour,
when I dont have the power,
To speak in your favour,
Okay! i am so cruel,
But i don't have the fuel,
to pursue you!
And then comes the hour,
I think nothing,
I feel nothing,
I feel numb,
I go through nothing,
And that is okay!

Aesthetic Self

Yes we are all the same,
yeah ! we all don't have the same strength to accept us as the same.

Do you have?
Then consider yourself the best. Will you?
Come on ! we will still consider us the second best.

Lets live in now and every now consider yourself the best !
yes! I say you are the best.
you say, i say, they say and everyone says it the one day.
yes! We are all the same!

Ah! we are all the best who sometimes do somehow the worst.
Come on ! we are all the same kind just somewhere differ in type,
But we are all the best to be the best!

Yes! we do the mistakes and thats okay !
We are not here to be perfect but the best,
Let's do what we want and see where we reach.

Yes we all are the same!
yes we all are the best!

Golden Mind

You have a golden mind,
That is full of gold.

Emotions and expressions is the real gold,
That is being so heavy.

Come on! Don't be scary,
Don't let it be hold by others.

Its not meant to be hold together,
Its only you the owner of that gold.

Think of that gold to come out,
And make yourself free from the burden.

Another miracles are in a way to happen very sudden,
Ah! enjoy all your beautiful version of yourself!

Be thyself!

Your Trueself

Hey dear mates!
We all are friends.

So whatever whenever god send,
Face it like a good friends.

Share everything whatever you have,
And care for everybody whoever you see.

Advice your friends always a good way,
Never you decide to go for a bad way.

Be loving be caring and be real to everybody,
This is all what i suggest you to be the best buddy.

Be your true self no matter what they do,
The way they pursued you need not to purse.

P.s: Do good to have good.

Nature

The nature is so wonderful,
Look around! it is so colorful.

Come away from your missions that are sorrowful,
Enjoy the beauty its so beautiful.

Winters are snowy and rainy,
Snow man and snow slide,
Ah! ride and pride.

Summer are raising and shining,
Bright and beautiful sight,
Ah! its sunny and funny.

Spring when its hot sun,
More longer days run,
Flowers bloom and no gloom.

Autumn when leaves fall,
Time for photographers to call,
Wow! hot and cold its equal.

Indeed nothing is more attractive,
It wakes you up, makes you active,
Its more than the word appreciative,

It gives the vibes so positive.

Loyals Are Not Fools

Just because she is being loyal to you.
Don't call her fool !
It won't make you cool !
But indeed you are so fool.

Now bear her insolent behaviour,
Now be your savior.
Now her words will be alot heavier,
Now-on you will be the broken heart carrier.

You teased her loyalty,
Now let her be disloyal,
You will wish to go under soil,
Always your blood will boil.

Then she will ask you,
Is she fool or cruel.

P.s: Being loyal is not being fool, Being cruel is not being cool.

Mind Readers

You already spoke my mind,
I gave up! You won gold cup.
I became speechless.
You did something miraculous. Yes!
When My mind was trying to clear some haphazard mess,
Oh God! I need to think about it somehow less.

God has really done injustice,
How could you read my mind,
why are then all other blind.
I need a best lawyer to find,
I need to be a fact speaker client.

You have an extra eye that can read my mind,
How could all other be blind!
Why can't me too find
What's going in your mind.
We are all blind,
How God could do this injustice.

Just Keep Flowing

Lets make our mood set !
Why to be upset?

So what if you are being sad?
No one will even try to make you glad.

Why to get mad?
Then better is to gad.

So what if you are being good?
They will still try to snesh your food.

Do what you want to do.
Why to make your head bow.
Go and choose your way with flow.

Dont let your name to be mentioned below,
Just work with flow.
Make yourself glow.
And Go slow...

All the society dramas are mellow.
Don't let you tears fell on your comforting pillow.
Just because the dramas are mellow!
Let it all go as it is.

Just go with flow.

Their faces will soon be yellow,
Seeing you glowing.
Seeing you flowing.

Worst to Best

O mankind! Don't be so unkind,
Don't make a mucky mind.

You are not meant to be a criminal,
Fix it in your mind to always remind.
Leave what you left behind,

Go and find kind people,
Don't act blind sheeple.

You are not really bad,
Its just the bad way you chose.
Go,Make people confuse,
And their thinking accuse,
Don't ever abuse.

Make them feed
Who are in need,
To do any good deed,
Is the seed to be succeed.

Be good enough now,
Forget the past somehow.
Maybe You were the worst,
Try now to be the best.

Believe Yourself

Sometimes you feel numb,
Sometimes you feel dumb,
They will wish you luck,
And show you good luck thumb,
But remember they are all nitrogen bomb.

Close your palm, breathe and sleep tight,
You will be calm and able to shine bright,
Fight for your every single right,
That is your right.

Have huge guts to fly your kite high,
To beat them by your words,
And say goodbye!
keep flying your kite high!

If you never lie,
Don't be afraid to die,
You are the gold not the fie,
Almighty's blessings are well-nigh.

Let out a sigh of relief,
And say goodbye to grief.
So what if god is taking your test,
Do believe for the best.

Work More To Dream Big

I can't wake up early in the morn,
I can't sleep early at the night.
For me its not right.

These habits of me are disturbing my routine,
Like smokers life by nicotine.
I need to change it for my best,
Only I can do it not the rest.

My dream are huge big,
I need to get up and start digging,
Nothing is gonna happen sitting here in the swing,
I need to reach there and achieve.

I need to find a way,
For that I might have to dig like I play,
I have nothing for now more to say,
For now, I need to go and find my way.

Be a Team

Better is to be together,
Try always, Not to scatter.
I promise you will never shatter,
All be one! Have fun.

One and one is two,
Two and two is four,
Four and four is eight,
Ah! Eight is a strong team.

It is way better than it seem,
And is many people's dream,
You all will always be joyous and never feel to scream,
You will together be a light beam.

Some of us agree with it sooner,
Some of us agree with it later,
You may always chatter
But they will flatter.
Be a team not each others hater.

P.s: Run after Loyals.

My Pen

Introducing my bestfriend,
Ah! That is my pen.

It writes my mind,
It writes mt heart,

It writes before even I say,
It knows what anyone else never may!

It takes all the heaviness from my heart away,
It makes me always feel okay.

It has a power to pendown words,
That are even more deep than see and ocean.

To the same we both agree,
To the same we both disagree.

I complete it,
It completes me.

When it is, them i am,
When i am, then it is!
So are we,
I and my pen are bestfriend.

P.s: Pen is the best friend forever who never decieves, make it your bestfriend.

Seperated Us

The roads seems clear for us to meet,
The thorns are between,
That are hurtful and hidden.

That was us! who planted the thorns,
We did things like newborns.
We acted like fawns.

We are living with regret,
That makes us upset,
But still don't move on and forget.

We lived years together,
And one day separated forever,
Jealous people were indeed clever.

I believed them, not you,
You believed them, not me,
How stupid we were, you see!

Maybe we both got,
That was not meant to sort,
Still we are just seperate not apart.

Either of us want to be old us,
Ugh! Ego is in between plus,
Neither of us showed focus,
Yes, we are both so cuss!

P.s: Ego Breaks Beautiful Bonds, never be egoistic

None Is Trust Worthy

You spread what you want,
But remember don't think I cannot,
What you did maybe you forgot,
But I cannot.

I don't make you realise,
But that was a sad demise,
Our friendship! despise,
Rumours you spread are surmise.

Everyone believed the words,
Because who spoke were you,
Whom I trust were just few,
Was this the gift you said you will give.

When you are around it has become hard to survive,
That trust is gonna never revive,
I am now where you can never arrive,
That me is no more alive.

Everytime Is Best To Do Best

So I force myself to sleep,
Then my nightmares make me weep,
Oops! I am tired,
It scares me so deep,
I see things so creepy,
That makes me no more sleepy.

I am afraid of nights,
They really are so impolite,
Maybe I am not alright,
But I don't have that bad sight,
Sometimes we all indeed fight to pass the night,
We hope some peace comes with light.

Then when the day comes,
What we all do we dumbs?

Peace comes with light
And light comes with a day?
To bring the light you don't have to lay!
Go, Work, and shout out to say,
You hustled to be this way!
You are now yourself the sunray!

Show What You are!

Always show you real face,
No matter how is the place.

Being fake is a big mistake,
It will give you a treacherous shake.

Show who you are and what you are,
That will take you near from the far.

You will be near the sky to touch the star,
Being real ones never fall,
Nor their image becomes small.

Ugh! Being fake is like a football,
They kick you right, right you fall,
They kick you left, left you fall,
So sad of being in their thrall.

Now get up, Be squal,
Be actual, Be Factual,
Being fake feels appalled,
Be real either here or there.

Do to show them you can,
Do not give them a chance to say you fled or jumped in a dam.

Feel Proud For Being a Girl

So what you are a girl,
Show them you can laugh loud,
Yes even in a huge crowd.
So what everyone is around,
Speak up and make them hear your sound,
Why to be in anyone's bound.

So what they try to make you feel down,
Chill down! Don't frown,
You too deserve a crown.
Be water, Make them drown,
Don't feel disowned and thrown,
You are the one who owns you.

You don't need a man to hold you up,
When they even can't make a tea cup,
You don't need a support of group,
You can yourself do setup,
Getup!
Work from sunup to sundown.

Unspoken Words

I have many ways to make you understand,
But the matter is still I can't!
Your why and my how,
All I have to resolve now.

Words are infinite to use,
But which ones should I choose,
Ugh! I am confused,
What if I refuse?
No,No! It clearly seems i am bemused.

Seeing myself puzzled in your why,
Arose another why,
Oh God will kill this guy!
Better is to say bye!

My frustration will now make me cry.
Neither I can lie nor I can fly,
My frustration will make you die,
Better is to leave this why at goodBye!

Persist To gain

See where you are,
And remember you can go so far,
Leave where they go and where they are,
How far he has gone and how far she has gone.
Don't focus on what they won.

There is a lot more to gain,
Its okay to fall, stand again,
It may give you pain,
But remember you can have your own plane.
Don't feel down, You too have brain.

None of us was born the big man,
Persist till you have alot of fan,
You are the best, mind it you can,
To reach the spot everyone has to ran,
You have to reach, make it your plan.

Family

Looking at my family gives me courage,
Always they make me listen to the new page,
That encourages me more.

They teach me how to face the world that is so savage,
They inspire me to do good deeds at a young age.

I am the reflection of my family.
Having a family is living so happily,
Hurray! I am succeeding rapidly.

Being away from my family,
Makes my mood ugly,
When I want them, I want them quickly,
I want them always and daily.

They are the ones I don't embarrass for being silly,
They are the ones who make me stronger rapidly,
They are the ones who make me happy quickly,
They are the ones who are restless for my reply.

Family supports in ups and downs,
They are your backbone in every different towns,
They love your every sounds.

They console you when everyone is against you,
What you feel they already knows,
They know you are true,
Let others review.

P.s: Family Provides Strength to fly high and touch the sky.

Home Sweet Home!

Home is ofcourse the best place,
Whether its a cottage or a palace.

Whether its in slum or smart area,
Its safe and peaceful like fishes have aquaria.

Its the place that truly belongs to you,
Its the place You belong from,
It has all the things you love.

It gathers your loved ones together.
It makes you feel better in every weather.
It gives you shelter from every monster.

It contains our good and bad times,
It reminds you your childhood crimes,
It makes you cry over memories sometimes.

Its the most comforting place in the universe,
We are not shy of doing things so perverse.
Indeed no place is better than home, its the place where you are grown.

P.s: Love your home even if its a cottage but is best because its yours.

Colors Of Fake People...

Sometimes you can't see,
What's going on in front of you.

After all still it's not so clear,
Why it seems so blur?
Oh! it's because of their new color.

They appear tricks, they are so tricky,
Tricks are appeared, you are so silly,
Then it hurts like eaten a lot of chilly.

After years they say one word sorry!
Don't confuse, read again your past dairy,
Remind the pain they gave you to carry.

Stay quite and far away,
That to come back they have no way,
Don't forget what they did the previous day.

Forgive them and stay free,
But for their friendship never agree,
Forgive them but never you forget!

Never welcome them back,
They are coming to play another game,

Kind of people never change!

Give them glimpses of your new version,
Take action to show them their position.

School

I used to think my school was a cage,
Every morn I used to tremble with rage,
But that was such a joyous age.

School days are the best,
Better than all other rest,
It hurts that we go there now just as a guest.

Lol! How I used to hate my uniform,
I miss the events on we used to perform,
When I remind I cry so hard like its coming a storm.

I miss all those people not only friends,
I want to live those days again with no end,
Ah! The precious time we together have spent.

How innocent we used to pretend,
After Loud guffaws behind the teacher,
Every school has its wonderful feature.

-Writing before a year. Should be written after a year.
Feeling sad year before for leaving the school another year.
#dpsbaramulla

Silence

Silence is a beautiful language,
That not your ears listen but your heart feels,
That not their tongue speaks but their eyes scream.

Being curious to see them furious may prove you wrong.

I believe no language more than the eyes scream is more true,
Sometimes, somewhere, Silence is the best answer rather to argue,
Sometimes silence is the language that you must pursue.

People who consider them accused for their silence must be removed.

Ofcourse silence is a beautiful language for beautiful mindsets,
Who not only see when they show themselves upset,
But feel it when they hide it and show off they are set.

Yes! Silence is a beautiful language that only beautiful mindsets get!

Burden Of Expectations

I carry the heaviness of how much my parents did for me,
I work all day in guilt for I am doing less and being free,
All I have to do is for what they agree, No way i can pursue for what they disagree.

The more they wish, the more I do,
Then the taunts they give when I argue,
Ah! That Inspires me more and pushes me forward in the queue I pursue.

I wish they don't have made me addicted to what I am,
Sometimes I want to jump in the deep dam,
I will do as much as I can, But hectic is what if I Can't!

The burden is so heavy, Its not so easy to carry,
I wish their expectations don't become the thorns in my way,
I can do a lot they say!
I believe I can, But what if those blessings are not written in my way.
Everyone will get stuck when its battle with luck!

Trying The Best

I want to be the best,
Not just good like the rest.

I want to be the Sparkling Sun,
Not the source of fun .

I want to always be positive and worthy of trust,
Not a cruelminded thats full of dirt and dust.

I want to be the one among chill ones,
Not among the stress taker dumbs.

I want you to want the great,
And I wish we don't be so lame!

Be sure not only to want,
Either achieve to be jaunty.

The Copy Cats

They will do what you did,
They will copy what you do,
Then you will do something,
Where they can't reach,
The level is so high, They can't fly this high.

They will try to tease you out,
They will try to push you back,
They will try to show you down,
They will try to come to your level,
But lol they will come following you.

Be inspired not jealous,
Do what you want,
Don't think you can't.
They will hate you,
They wish to kill you.

P.s: Keep everyone aside, keep working for more success.

Be a Great Personality

Your words describe your mindsets,
Your mindsets describe your personality.

Think before you speak,
So no regrets would take place after you speak.

Speak positive,
See positive,
Think positive,
Be positive.

Spread positivity to make yourself a great personality,
Inspire and motivate them to be positive.

Try to change negativity by your positivity,
Give them love where you get hate,
Your love will make them tired of giving hate.

Be broadthinker and a good speaker,
Not just a good speaker,
But a great listener as well.

Mom and Dad

I love all the pictures,
You are captured in.

I love all the seconds and minutes,
I have spent with you.

I love every that place,
Where I find you.

I love all the people,
You are in love with.

I love everyone you love,
Because i love you.

This is the best poem i have written.
Because its for my mom and dad.
Who calm me down when I get mad.

Who make me happy whenever I am sad.
Who teach me good when I do bad.
Who are the reason why I am glad!

I thank God, I thank God.

What Love Paid!

Everyday she called that bird,
And one day he really heard.
But not even spoke a word,
He was really looking so tired.

She really loved him alot
And one day she saw him in a boat,
Then he jumped over and float.
To save the drowning goat.

She really appreciate the efforts he put,
He is so brave but what about her crave.
Why can't he save her from the grave,
She is even ready to be his slave.

She really can live thousand years by his single wave,
But the grief is not even a glance he gave.
Then came the day, She really passed away,
This was what her love paid.

I went to see and shame that bird,
There I saw him laid in a cage.
The story has been added a new page,
He really loved her more, from his heart's core.

He wanted to see her free,
Not to engage her with him in a cage.
Both of their love lead to death,
None side love was less.

They will meet in the heaven,
And together punish the demon.

P.s: Donot kill yourself after love.

Make Yourself a History

Make it your important mission,
That your name must be alive,
For decades and decades after you die,
Make yourself a history,
Nothing more than this is a great victory.

Printed by Libri Plureos GmbH in Hamburg,
Germany